Comparing Past and Present

Going to the Doctor

Rebecca Rissman

Heinemann
LIBRARY

Chicago, Illinois

© 2014 Heinemann Library
an imprint of Capstone Global Library, LLC
Chicago, Illinois

To contact Capstone Global Library please phone 800-747-4992, or visit our website www.capstonepub.com

Edited by Rebecca Rissman, Daniel Nunn, and
    Catherine Veitch
Designed by Philippa Jenkins
Picture research by Elizabeth Alexander
Production by Helen McCreath
Originated by Capstone Global Library Ltd

Library of Congress Cataloging-in-Publication Data
Rissman, Rebecca.
  Going to the doctor / Rebecca Rissman.
    pages cm.—(Comparing past and present)
  Includes bibliographical references and index.
  ISBN 978-1-4329-8992-7 (hb)—ISBN 978-1-4329-9026-8 (pb)
1. Medical care—History—Juvenile literature. 2. Physicians—Juvenile literature. 3. Health—Juvenile literature. I. Title.
  R130.5.R57 2014
  610—dc23   2013012544

Image Credits
Alamy: jozef mikietyn, 11, 23, Old Visuals, 8, Tetra Images, 7, YAY Media AS, 5, Yogi Black, 6; Getty Images: A. R. Coster, 4, Bettmann, 18, Fox Photos, cover (right), 10, Halfdark, 17, 23, Harrison, 16, 23, SelectStock, cover (left), Vintage Images, 12; Mary Evans Picture Library: Sueddeutsche Zeitung Photo, 14; Shutterstock: CandyBox Images, 13, mangostock, 15, Monkey Business Images, 21, wavebreakmedia, 19, 23; Superstock: 4X5 Collection/Devaney Collection, back cover, 22, Blend Images, 9, ClassicStock, 20

We would like to thank Nancy Harris and Diana Bentley for their invaluable help in the preparation of this book.

Contents

Comparing the Past and Present

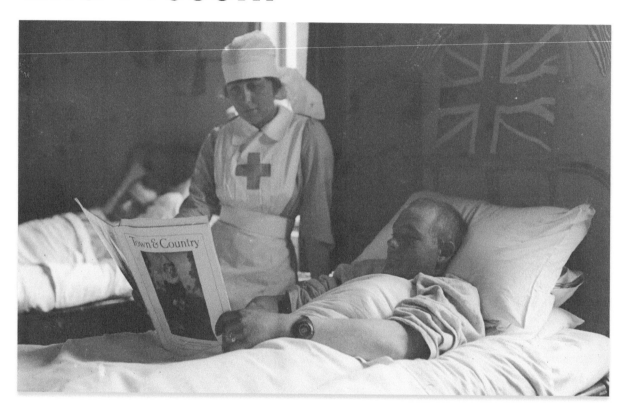

Things in the past have already happened.

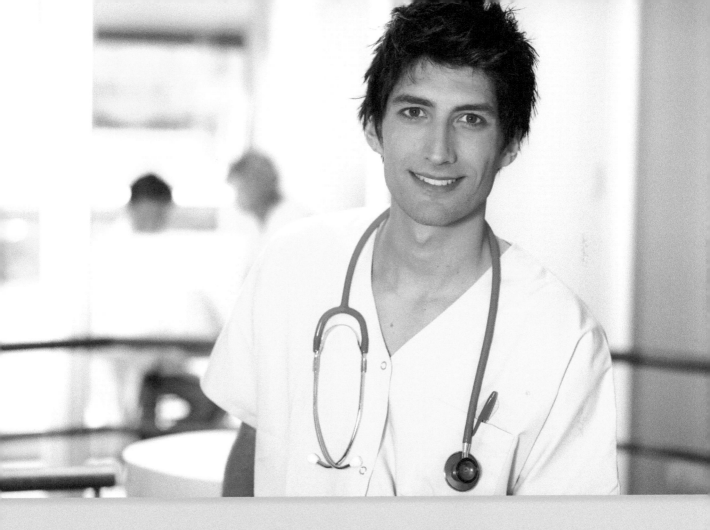

Things in the present are happening now.

5

Going to the doctor has changed over time.

The way people go to the doctor today is very different from the past.

Seeing the Doctor

In the past, some doctors visited the homes of sick people.

Today, most people see a doctor
at a clinic or hospital.

Getting to the Doctor

In the past, some people went a long way to see the doctor.

Today, most people live close to a clinic or hospital.

In the past, some sick people went to the hospital in ambulance carts.

Today, some sick people get to
a hospital in an ambulance.

Medicine

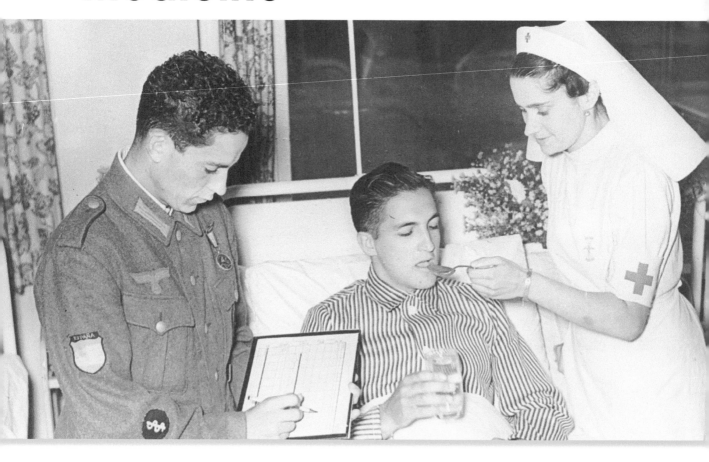

In the past, doctors had few medicines to help sick people.

Today, there are many medicines
to help people get better.

Hospitals

patients

In the past, hospitals were made up of large rooms. Many patients stayed in the same room.

Today, hospitals are made up of many small rooms. Fewer patients stay in the same room.

Doctors and Nurses

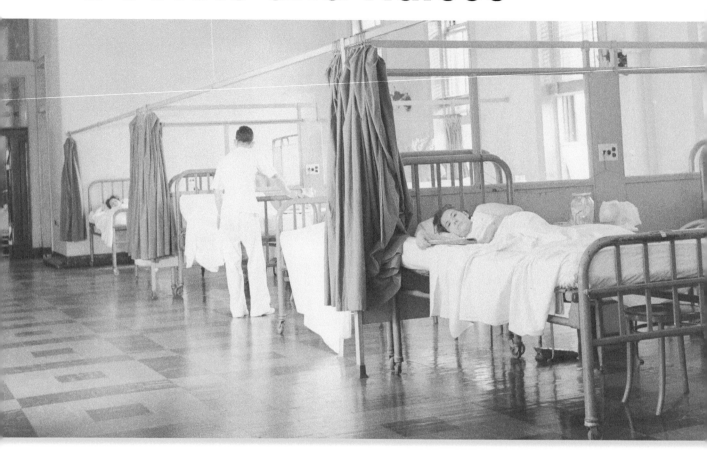

In the past, hospitals had fewer doctors.

Today, hospitals have many doctors.

In the past, nurses and doctors helped patients at the hospital.

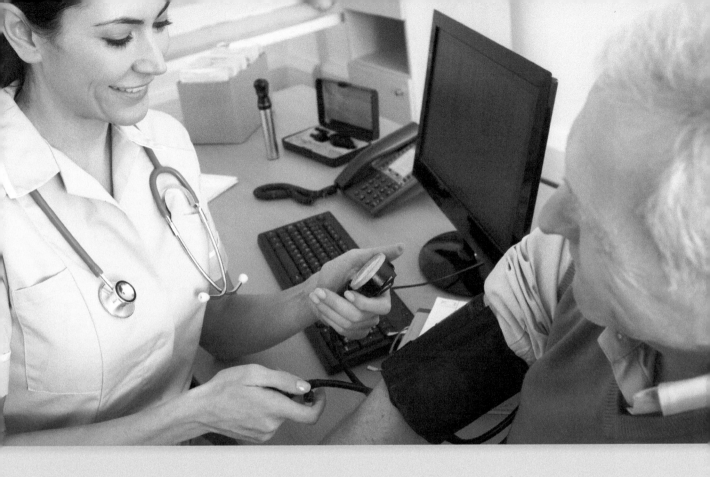

Today, nurses and doctors also
help patients at the hospital.

Then and Now

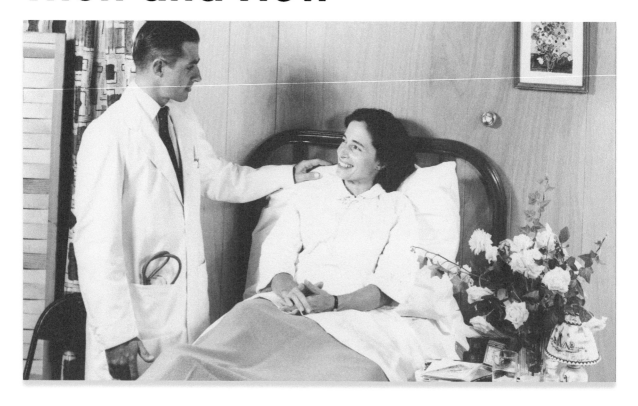

In the past, doctors did their best to help sick patients. Today, doctors still do their best to help sick patients.

Picture Glossary

 clinic place where doctors see their patients

 hospital place where doctors and nurses work to care for patients

 nurse person who works in a hospital helping to care for patients

 patient person visiting a doctor for medicine or medical care

Index

Note to Parents and Teachers

Before reading

Teach children about the difference between the past and present. Explain to children that things that have already happened are in the past. To help them understand this concept, ask children to tell you about what they ate for breakfast. Then, explain to them that their breakfast happened in the past. Tell children that your conversation is happening in the present.

After reading

- Explain to children that the way people visit the doctor has changed over time. Ask children to describe their last visit to a doctor. Encourage them to think about driving to the doctor's office, whether they saw a nurse, and what the office looked like.

- Ask children to look at the images on pages 12—13. Can they think of any ways the images are different? Can they think of why it might be helpful to get to the hospital quickly?

- Show children the image on page 15. Explain that today, many medicines exist to help people heal from different sicknesses. Ask children how life in the past might have been more difficult with fewer medicines.